MW01479157

CITY CRITTERS

YOUR NEIGHBOR THE ALLEY CAT

GREG ROZA

WINDMILL BOOKS

New York

Published in 2012 by Windmill Books, An Imprint of Rosen Publishing
29 East 21st Street, New York, NY 10010

Copyright © 2012 by Windmill Books, An Imprint of Rosen Publishing

All rights reserved. No part of this book may be reproduced in any form without permission in writing from the publisher, except by a reviewer.

First Edition

Editor: Jennifer Way
Layout Design: Greg Tucker

Photo Credits: Cover, pp. 4, 5, 6, 7, 8, 9, 10, 11, 12, 13, 14, 16 (top), 17, 18, 19, 20–21, 22 Shutterstock.com; p. 15 © www.iStockphoto.com/tbradford; p. 16 (bottom) © www.iStockphoto.com/Uygar Ozel.

Library of Congress Cataloging-in-Publication Data

Roza, Greg.
 Your neighbor the alley cat / by Greg Roza. — 1st ed.
   p. cm. — (City critters)
 Includes index.
 ISBN 978-1-4488-4999-4 (library binding) — ISBN 978-1-4488-5127-0 (pbk.) —
ISBN 978-1-4488-5128-7 (6-pack)
 1. Feral cats—Juvenile literature. I. Title.
 SF450.R69 2012
 636.8—dc22
                           2010052264

Manufactured in the United States of America

For more great fiction and nonfiction, go to www.windmillbooks.com

CPSIA Compliance Information: Batch #BS2011WM: For Further Information contact Windmill Books, New York, New York at 1-866-478-0556

CONTENTS

WHERE DO ALLEY CATS COME FROM?	4
LIFE WITH CATS	6
HUNTING FOR DINNER	8
TOMS AND MOLLIES	10
KITTENS	12
WHERE'S HOME?	14
ALLEY CATS IN YOUR NEIGHBORHOOD	16
THE HARD LIFE	18
ALLEY CATS AS PETS?	20
URBAN SAFARI	22
GLOSSARY	23
INDEX	24
WEB SITES	24

WHERE DO ALLEY CATS COME FROM?

From the deepest ocean to the tallest mountain, wild animals live just about everywhere on Earth. Just because you live in a town or city does not mean there are not wild animals nearby. If you live in a city, chances are good that there are alley cats in your neighborhood.

Alley cats are also called stray cats.

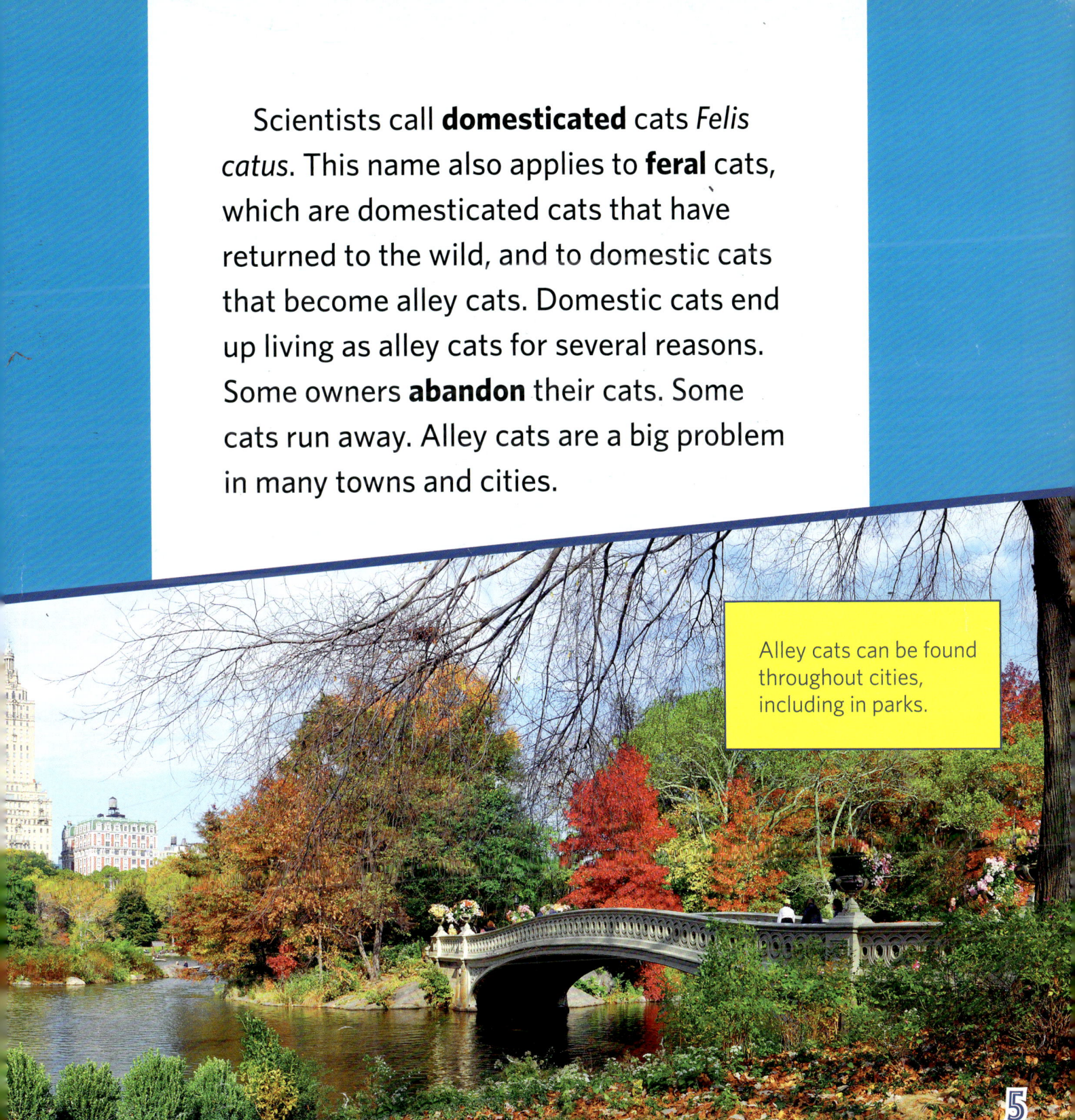

Scientists call **domesticated** cats *Felis catus*. This name also applies to **feral** cats, which are domesticated cats that have returned to the wild, and to domestic cats that become alley cats. Domestic cats end up living as alley cats for several reasons. Some owners **abandon** their cats. Some cats run away. Alley cats are a big problem in many towns and cities.

Alley cats can be found throughout cities, including in parks.

LIFE WITH CATS

Cats began living with people thousands of years ago. This likely occurred around the time that farming began to provide **surplus** food. As natural hunters, cats caught mice and rats that were eating stored grain. People began to feed and care for cats so that

Cats are common house pets. There are about 94 million pet cats in the United States!

they would continue to kill mice and rats for them. Soon after, cats became domesticated. Today, cats are kept as pets throughout the world.

Domestic cats, also called house cats, are **mammals**. If you have a cat, you know that they can be curious and playful. Outside the safety of a home, though, curiosity can get a cat into trouble.

Cats come in many colors and patterns. Striped cats (right) have a tabby pattern. Black and white cats (left) are sometimes called tuxedo cats.

HUNTING FOR DINNER

Cats are **carnivores**, which means they are meat eaters. Alley cats may hunt for small to medium-sized animals. They eat mostly **rodents**, but they will also catch and eat fish, lizards, birds, bats, and bugs. Cats in towns and cities generally do not have trouble finding **prey**.

Kittens learn hunting skills, such as stalking and pouncing, through play.

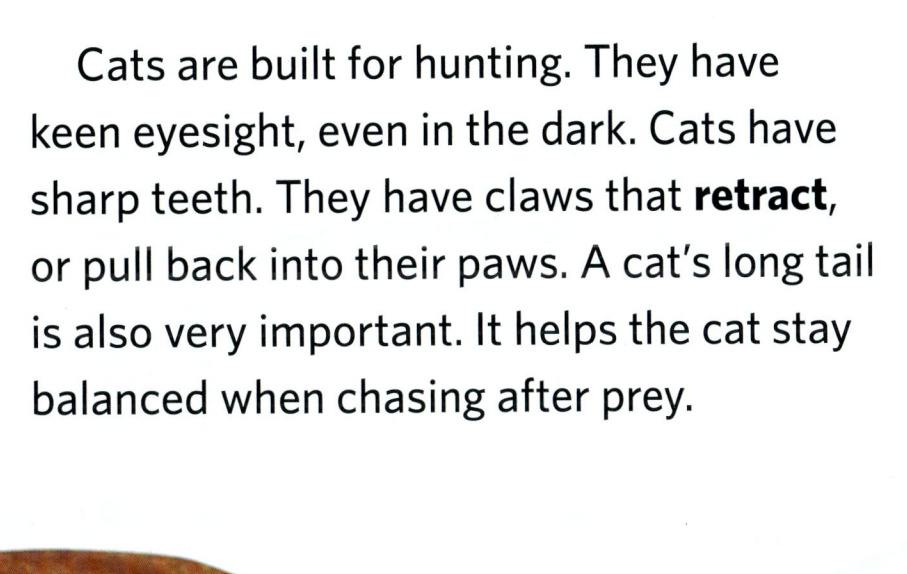

Cats are built for hunting. They have keen eyesight, even in the dark. Cats have sharp teeth. They have claws that **retract**, or pull back into their paws. A cat's long tail is also very important. It helps the cat stay balanced when chasing after prey.

When cats are hunting, they crouch and keep their eyes on their prey.

TOMS AND MOLLIES

Alley cats generally weigh less than house cats. They can weigh up to 11 pounds (5 kg). Male cats are called toms and female cats are called mollies. Toms are generally larger than mollies. Adult male and female cats can **mate** at any

A female cat that has kittens is called a queen.

time during the year, as long as they have enough food and shelter. Alley cats are generally ready to mate at between four and seven months old. Females can have as many as three **litters** a year.

Female cats take care of their young. Male cats do not help in raising the kittens.

Male cats may fight each other over mates.

KITTENS

About 63 to 65 days after mating, a female cat gives birth to a litter of kittens. A litter generally has between four and six kittens. Newborn kittens are blind, deaf, and toothless. They have a coat of fine fur. They spend their time snuggled together with their mother. After about two weeks, the

The mother cat feeds her kittens with her milk. This is called nursing.

kittens can see and hear. They then begin to explore their world.

Kittens drink their mother's milk for about eight or nine weeks. They spend much of their time playing and copying adult cats. By five months old, the kittens have lost their baby teeth and fur and have grown adult teeth and fur.

Kittens learn through play. The toy shown here can help these kittens learn hunting skills.

WHERE'S HOME?

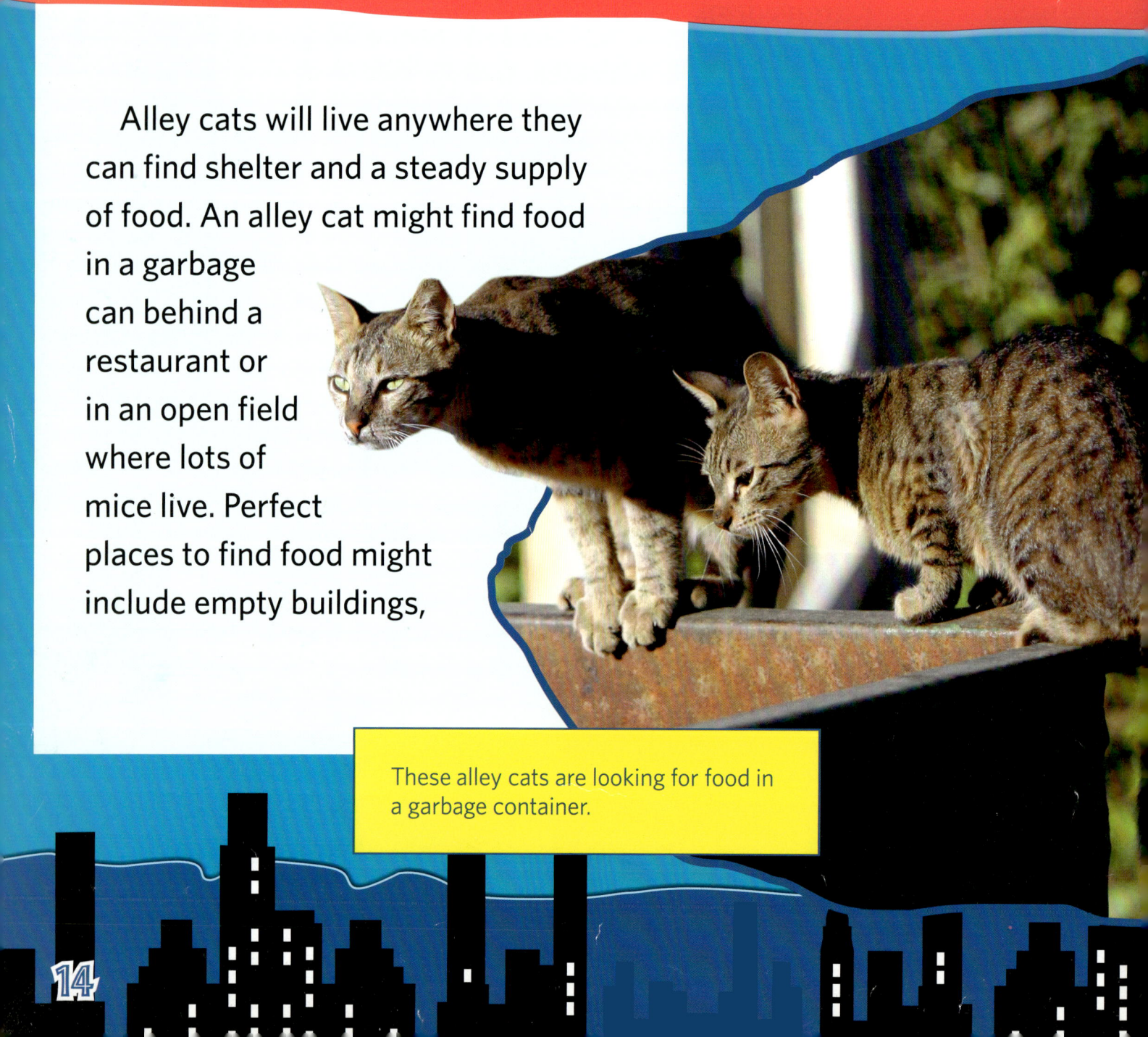

Alley cats will live anywhere they can find shelter and a steady supply of food. An alley cat might find food in a garbage can behind a restaurant or in an open field where lots of mice live. Perfect places to find food might include empty buildings,

These alley cats are looking for food in a garbage container.

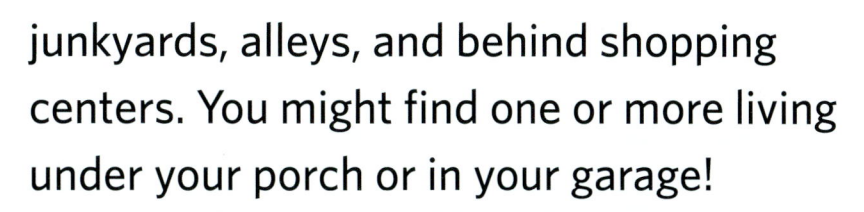

junkyards, alleys, and behind shopping centers. You might find one or more living under your porch or in your garage!

Alley cats often move from one place to another when food runs low. Since cats **breed** so quickly, it is common to find a dozen, or even dozens, of cats all living in the same place.

Sometimes several alley cats will make their home in the same place.

ALLEY CATS IN YOUR NEIGHBORHOOD

Alley cats are often skinny and afraid of people. If you ever find a well-fed, affectionate cat in your neighborhood, chances are good that it is a lost house cat.

Alley cats may make a mess of your garbage cans at night if you do not put the lids on tightly.

Cats are good hunters. They help keep the number of pests in your neighborhood low.

It is important to get pet cats **neutered** or **spayed**. This helps keep down the number of unwanted cats.

Mother alley cats like to hide their kittens in out-of-the-way places. You might find a family of cats living in your garage or shed.

Some groups set traps to catch alley cats so they can be neutered. Some of these cats are friendly enough to be adopted by caring families.

Male cats mark their territories with solid and liquid waste.

THE HARD LIFE

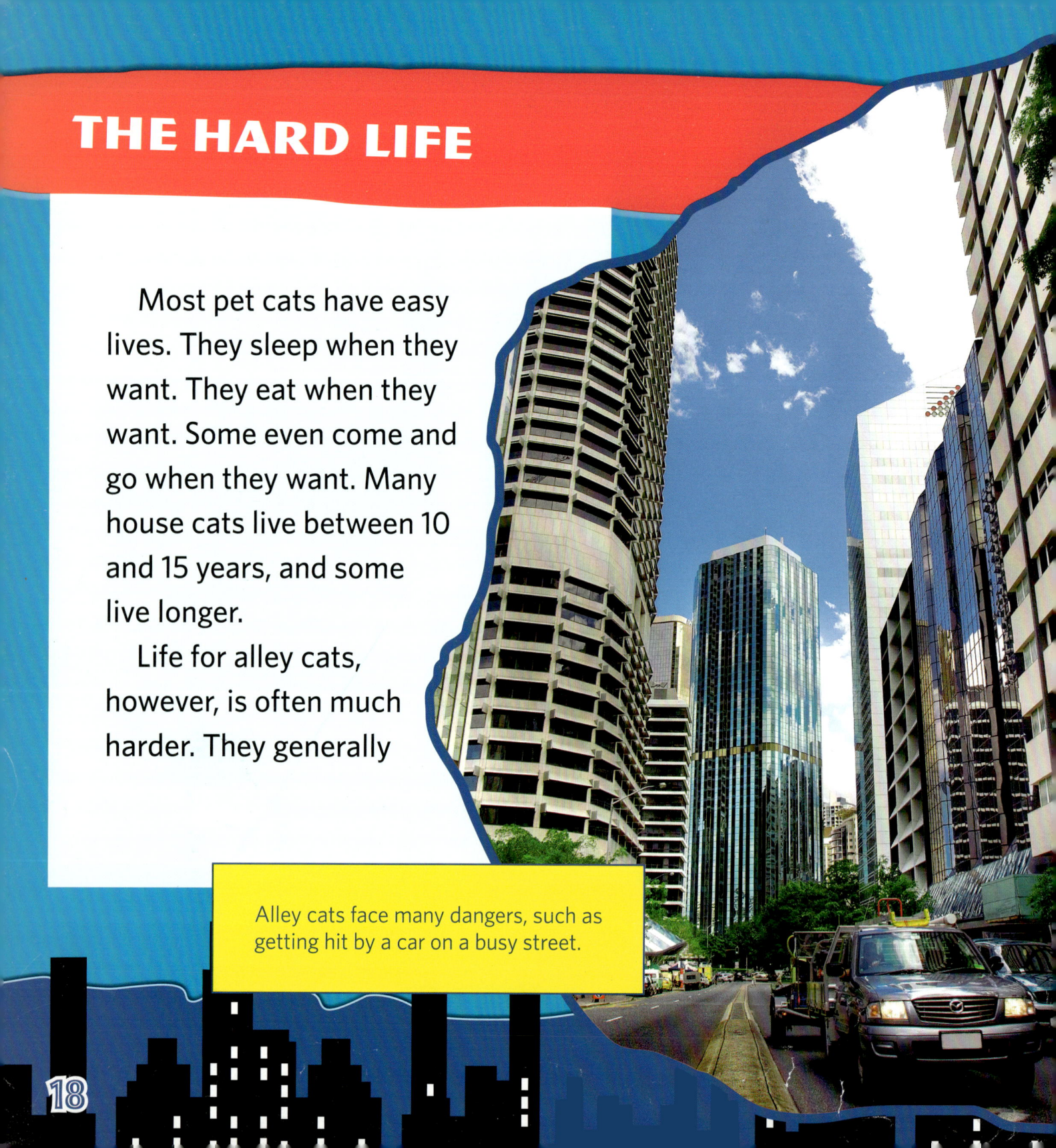

Most pet cats have easy lives. They sleep when they want. They eat when they want. Some even come and go when they want. Many house cats live between 10 and 15 years, and some live longer.

Life for alley cats, however, is often much harder. They generally

Alley cats face many dangers, such as getting hit by a car on a busy street.

Many alley cats are sick, hungry, or unable to find a safe place to sleep.

live for only two or three years. Alley cats cannot always find warm places to sleep or good meals. They are often sick or carrying fleas that cause diseases. Their greatest enemies are dogs and people. Since cats mate at any time of the year, overpopulation is a big problem.

ALLEY CATS AS PETS?

It is important to be careful around alley cats. Many are not used to people. They may bite and scratch. Some have diseases that are harmful to people, such as **rabies**. Never try to pick up an alley cat.

Some alley cats can become house cats. Before an alley cat comes to live

Before an alley cat can be adopted, it needs to visit a veterinarian for a check-up.

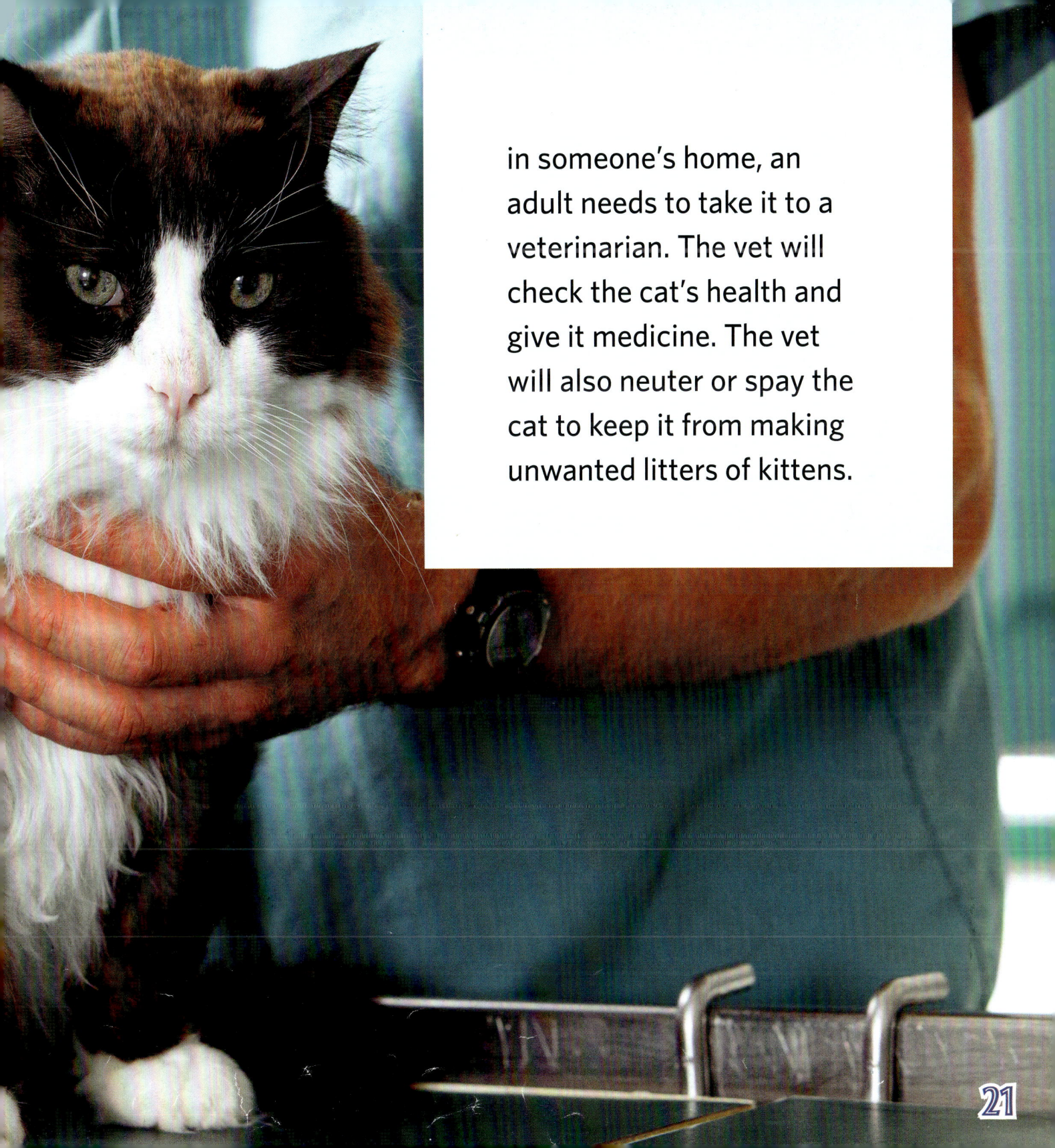

in someone's home, an adult needs to take it to a veterinarian. The vet will check the cat's health and give it medicine. The vet will also neuter or spay the cat to keep it from making unwanted litters of kittens.

URBAN SAFARI

Whether they are friendly or not, there are signs you can look for to tell if alley cats live in your neighborhood. Have you noticed a decrease in the number of birds in your neighborhood? Alley cats might be eating them! Unlike house cats, which bury their waste, alley cats will leave their solid waste unburied. They do this to mark their territories.

Cats like to climb trees so that they can watch what is going on on the ground.

Cats like to sit in high spots to see what is going on around them. You might find cat prints on cars. These are all signs that you have alley cats for neighbors.

GLOSSARY

ABANDON (uh-BAN-dun) To leave something without planning to come back to get it.

BREED (BREED) To make babies.

CARNIVORES (KAHR-neh-vorz) Animals that eat other animals.

DOMESTICATED (duh-MES-tih-kayt-ed) Raised to live with people.

FERAL (FER-al) An animal that used to live with people but that has gone back to the wild.

LITTERS (LIH-terz) Groups of kittens born to the same mother at the same time.

MAMMALS (MA-mulz) Warm-blooded animals that have a backbone and hair, breathe air, and feed milk to their young.

MATE (MAYT) To come together to make babies.

NEUTERED (NOO-terd) Fixed so that a male animal cannot make babies.

PREY (PRAY) An animal that is hunted by another animal for food.

RABIES (RAY-beez) A deadly illness that wild animals can carry.

RETRACT (rih-TRAKT) To draw back.

RODENTS (ROH-dents) Animals with gnawing teeth, such as mice.

SPAYED (SPAYD) Fixed a female animal so that it cannot have babies.

SURPLUS (SUR-plus) More than enough.

INDEX

C
city, 4–5, 8

F
farming, 6
food, 6, 11, 14–15

G
garbage can(s), 14, 16
grain, 6

H
hunters, 6, 17

K
kittens, 11–13, 17, 21

L
litter(s), 11–12, 21

M
mammals, 7
mice, 6–7, 14
mountain, 4

N
name, 5
neighborhood, 4, 16–17, 22

O
ocean, 4
owners, 5

P
people, 6, 16, 19–20
prey, 8–9
problem, 5, 19

R
rabies, 20
rats, 6–7
rodents, 8

S
safety, 7
scientists, 5

T
town(s), 4–5, 8

WEB SITES

For Web resources related to the subject of this book, go to: www.windmillbooks.com/weblinks and select this book's title.